The Hustler's Guide to Golf

Great Golf Betting Games and How to Win Them Every Time

by Jay Willi

Illustrations by Barrie Maguire

Andrews McMeel Publishing

Kansas City

D1563628

www.andrewsmcmeel.com

ISBN: 0-8362-5188-1

The Hustler's Guide to Golf is produced by becker&mayer!

Art direction by Simon Sung
Designed by Amy Redmond
Edited by Lissa Wolfendale

FOREWORD

The Bad Golfers Association was established to serve, support, and inform the average golfer. The BGA defines the average golfer to be "someone whose love of the game exceeds his or her ability to play it." That pretty much describes every golfer in the universe. The BGA is not an association for hackers, it is an association for less gifted golfers. In other words, the BGA is not the PGA. But like the PGA, BGA members appreciate the betting abilities of great golfers like Titanic Thompson, Sam Snead, Lee Trevino, Al Besselink, Bobby Riggs, and Lanny Wadkins.

Building upon the strong foundation of *Golf Dirty Tricks*, the bible for golfers who from time to time need an edge, *The Hustler's Guide to Golf: Great Golf Betting Games and How to Win Them Every Time* teaches players how to capitalize on the edges available in every golf betting game. There's nothing like the adrenaline rush that comes from a large wager on a game, a hole, or a shot. Like life, golf often isn't fair. Why should golf gambling be any different?

If you would like to join the BGA and receive a membership card, the rule book, and the quarterly BGA newsletter, send $9.95 to: BGA World Headquarters, 4520 Main Street, Kansas City, MO 64111.

Money and the game of golf are inseparable. You reaffirm that principle every time you mark your ball with a coin.

Having $20 on the line puts an electric charge into a game of golf that makes the normal Saturday morning foursome far more interesting than its usual cart ride through the park.

When Dick and Murray have a wager with Mike and Lester, the tensile strength of friendship is severely tested. No matter how many birthday parties you've attended, how many barbecues or Christmas Eve affairs, your friends are officially your enemies when it comes to golf gambling. You are completely authorized to hate them, even over nothing more than a $2 bet.

And there's even more drama in making wagers with strangers—this is a challenge to your very ego. Do you have the courage to tee off into the unknown? Do you have the inner strength to make that five-footer under the piercing glare of a stranger's eyes? Are you tough enough?

Getting a game with strangers means being both aggressive and subtle. Don't dress flashy. Don't wear your St. Andrews Old Course shirt under your Augusta National sweater. Don't wear $300 shoes or $200 wool slacks, even if you happen to favor them. Wear an old, faded polo, khakis, and white socks with year-old spikes that have been cleaned once a month. On the other hand, if someone wearing flashy attire offers you a bet, take it. You can be sure he has a good job and an overextended ego.

As the famous late freeloader George Low once said: "Give me a millionaire with a bad backswing and I can have a very pleasant day."

Now we would like to tell you about golf games you can play and ways you can improve your chances of winning and of filling your wallet. No guarantees, mind you. Just some ideas on getting the edge on your opponents—sometimes in ways that would make a golf rules official blush, if not throw up all over his white bucks. Hey, life isn't fair, so why should golf gambling be? Take any edge you can get, because there is only one certainty: If you don't take it, the other guy will.

The Betting Personalities

The Pigeon

Gawd, the golf world loves a Pigeon. This is a player who consistently overestimates his own abilities while inexplicably underestimating his handicap. He'll often have the best clothes and the best clubs, and will have played at the best courses—a fact you quickly surmise by all the Pinehurst and Pebble Beach and Winged Foot tags still clinging to his 100-pound, genuine ostrich leather golf bag. With a Pigeon, the idea is not to drool (you'll be eating squab soon enough). Let the Pigeon do virtually all of the talking. Let him suggest the games and the stakes. All you have to do is make casual remarks such as, "It seems like such a terrific day to be playing for only $5," or, "It's traditional at this club that we play a few side games," or, "You can press at any time." Don't frighten the Pigeon, just nudge him a bit, and you'll have a mouthful of feathers by day's end.

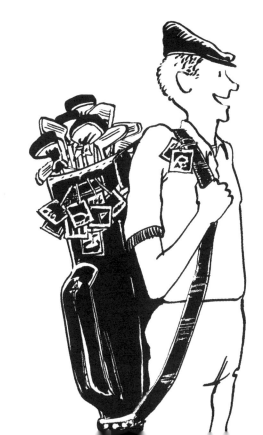

Two-Dollar Dave

This is a guy who will always gamble, as long as the bet never exceeds the standard $2 Nassau where the most he's likely to lose is $10. He has a wallet sealed tighter than the hatch on a space shuttle and still thinks the minimum wage is $1.25. He wouldn't bet $20 if he could win $2,000. You don't need this guy, but his type is virtually unavoidable. You can probably figure him out before you even reach the first tee, because he'll never say anything about a wager until you get there. If you have to bring it up, he'll immediately respond, "Okay, $2 sounds good to me." If you are sharing a caddie, you can also spot this guy by the fact that the caddie wants to talk to you all day long and make sure you have the right yardage and the right club. This is because Two-Dollar Dave is a $2 tipper, and caddies will do anything to make sure they get a lavish tip from you.

Frenetic Phil

You don't want this guy as a partner and you only want him as an opponent if you are sure you can take him for at least $100. He talks all the time and wants to give you advice on everything from the line of your putt to the lining of your blazer. Even as you line up the simplest ten-footer, he'll be over your shoulder saying, "Now this breaks about a ball and a half left to right. It's looks more uphill than it really is. The cup is crowned a little bit, so play less break and hit it harder so that it doesn't fall off at the lip. You're going with the grain, so maybe don't hit as hard as you think you should." If you didn't have ten bucks riding on the hole, you would bury your putter in his skull. If you're playing a foursome and he's your opponent, be sure to make nice to him all the time and say how important it is for a partner to be involved in the decision making. This is guaranteed to have him all over his own partner, which will annoy and distract him. Just hope he doesn't bury his putter in Frenetic Phil's head before the round is over.

The Quiet Quinn

Be careful of guys who don't talk too much—who don't suggest the bets or the match but agree to almost any wager too easily. A Quiet Quinn can be the type of guy that lets you hang yourself with your own rope. If he's been pretty quiet in the clubhouse and the practice tee, start the bidding low when setting the amount of the wagers. If you suggest $5 and he says, "I wouldn't mind playing for $10, if that's okay with you guys," all the while looking away from you in an embarrassed, humble sort of way, don't take the bet unless you are getting strokes from the guy or know that you have the right partner. Actually, a Quiet Quinn is the ideal gambler and you can take lessons from this personality type, especially when it comes to betting with strangers. Push the bets up by suggestion rather than demand. Never say, "I won't play for less than $20," because that will automatically become the most your opponent will let you play for. Quiet Quinns let the ego of their opponent work for them.

One-Iron Jack

It's always a good idea to look in the other player's bag before making a wager. If you see a one-iron in there, be very, very careful. Lee Trevino has always maintained that only God and Jack Nicklaus can hit a one-iron. Players don't carry a one-iron unless they can hit them. Of course, a one-iron carrier might be a little egomaniacal, but don't count on it. What you really should do before deciding on a wager (and most important, the handicap strokes) is to see this guy swing. Suggest that you hit a few on the range. You will, of course, make sure you don't strike the ball too solidly. You will also ask to see the one-iron, take a terrible swing with it, then hand it back and say, "Show me how to use this thing, won't you?" Negotiate for the most strokes you can get and don't play many side bets with a One-Iron Jack.

The Sacred Betting Rules

THE SACRED BETTING RULES

(1) Don't be afraid to take advantage of your best friend.

(2) Don't be afraid to annoy your worst enemy. He'll play worse.

(3) Bets are paid off in cash, in the locker room. Do not exchange money on the eighteenth green or in the dining room.

(4) A bet may be paid off as part or whole of the bar tab after a round.

THE SACRED BETTING RULES

(5) Only take markers from someone whose phone number is in your black book.

(6) All markers must be paid off by year's end (for tax purposes).

(7) Do not covet your best friend's partner.

8   Don't offer to cover an unexpectedly large, lost wager with
your partner's gold Rolex—or at least ask him first.

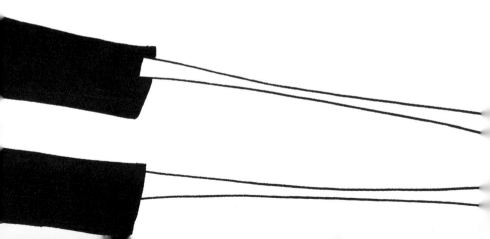

(9) Always, always, always shake hands on the eighteenth green, win or lose. (If you must punch somebody in the face, offer to show him the new mower in the superintendent's barn.)

(10) Never make a bet that exceeds your alimony payment.

Blasphemous
Cheating Guidelines

BLASPHEMOUS CHEATING GUIDELINES

(1) On a hole with a blind tee shot, make sure to offer to go up and check to see if it's okay to hit. Out of sight, toss a ball down the left or right side of the fairway into an "A" position for a good approach shot. Just whack a tee shot any ole way, then when you get up to the fairway, say, "Well, this must be my lucky day." (You could put a ball in the hole on those rare blind approach shots to the green, but that might be a bit much for even the most gullible player to swallow.)

BLASPHEMOUS CHEATING GUIDELINES

(2) Since you seldom need to use all fourteen clubs anyhow, leave out
the long iron you can't hit with and substitute an extra driver with
a 72-inch shaft. You'll never hit it, but it will sure come in handy
when you're taking relief. Two club lengths with a six-foot shaft is
twelve feet, and that will get you in good position every time.

(3) Practice coughing. It's your ace-in-the-hole—if you don't overuse it. Make sure you start coughing in the clubhouse before the round, to establish your allergic reaction to grass.

(4) When you're on the green and your opponent has his back turned, make sure to take a couple of steps on the line of his putt right in front of the cup. Scuff your foot, quietly. Make sure to repair the damage before going on to the next hole.

(5) Drop an extra club in your opponent's bag before the start of the round, giving him one more than the allowed fourteen. If you're trailing at a critical stage, call him for carrying too many clubs.

(6) Get to know the greens superintendent well. There's an old story about how Ben Hogan, tired of losing bets to members of the Shady Oaks Golf Club who got a bunch of strokes from him in matches, went out one morning with the greens superintendent and had every pin cut in the front left corner of the greens. Since most players hit the ball left to right and Hogan could draw it right to left, he had the advantage on every approach shot. He won every bet that day. In big-money situations, have the superintendent help tailor the course to your game and away from an opponent's—for a piece of the action, of course.

(7) If you're playing winter rules (where you can legally move the ball with your club for a better lie), carry a few lime Life Savers in your pocket. You could surreptitiously drop one near your ball and then tee the ball up on it.

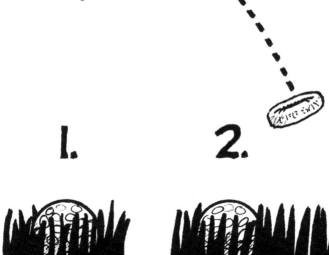

1.

2.

(8) Always carry a minimum of four coins in your pocket, and make sure that at least one is a fifty-cent piece. They come in handy for jingling just as your opponent is making his putting stroke.

(9) Get to know the printer of your club's scorecards. You might be able to ask him for a special run, one that subtly adjusts the holes on which the handicap shots are awarded. If you are giving away strokes to an opponent, you can give him a card that shifts those strokes from the more difficult holes to the easier ones. If you are getting strokes, you can shift them to the holes where you always have the most difficulty.

(10) Get your hands on some blank handicap cards. Then when you add an extra stroke or two to your handicap, you'll have the card handy to whip out to answer an opponent who asks, "Are you sure you're only a 15?" On the bogus card you can also alter the Slope Rating of your home course. The Slope Rating is a measure of the relative difficulty of your course as opposed to every other course. Always make sure the Slope Rating of your course shows that it is very easy. That way you automatically get more handicap strokes on a tougher course. And when your opponent asks, "Is Winged Foot really easier than Rabbit Run?" you'll have the official document to prove it.

(11) Wear a lightweight watch with a shiny face. Use it to angle the sun's reflection at your opponent's eyes. Just a quick flash, mind you. He'll be distracted without actually knowing what's happening to him. Practice this at home by trying to hit a spot on your house's exterior while pretending to be painting.

(12) Always talk to yourself, which is a great way to be actually getting into your opponent's head without ever addressing him directly. "Okay, self, remember this green is a lot faster than the others," or, "C'mon, self, this shot always plays longer than it looks," or, "Jeez, self, you put three balls in the water last week so play it really safe." The object, of course, is to talk your opponent into making exactly the wrong play.

BLASPHEMOUS CHEATING GUIDELINES

(13) On par-3 holes, if you are hitting first, take two clubs to the tee with you, one of which is at least three clubs short of what you—and your opponent—need to hit. Hold the sole of that club up in the air and indicate that's the one you will be hitting. Then say, "Oops, better take one extra." In fact, you will take another club that is at least two extra, and just right for the shot. If your opponent takes the one extra off the club you had originally shown him, he's dogmeat.

(14) Carry petroleum jelly in your bag, disguised in a tube of suntan lotion. If your tee shots are going askew, you can cut down the rotation on the ball that causes a slice or a hook by putting a light smear on the face of the driver.

(15) When you have a short putt, pretend there is a ball mark, or even two, in your line right near the cup. In the process of repairing them you can use your putter to stamp down the turf in front of the cup, allowing you to create a funnel right into the heart of the jar.

(16) When you are playing on rainy days and using the "lift, clean, and replace" rule, hit souped-up balls off the tee for extra distance. Then you can lift, clean, and replace them, deftly, with your normal ball for the approach shot to the green and for putting. On par 5s, hit the souped-up ball twice. Have your second ball already in a towel when you clean the first ball. It's a move virtually no one will ever detect.

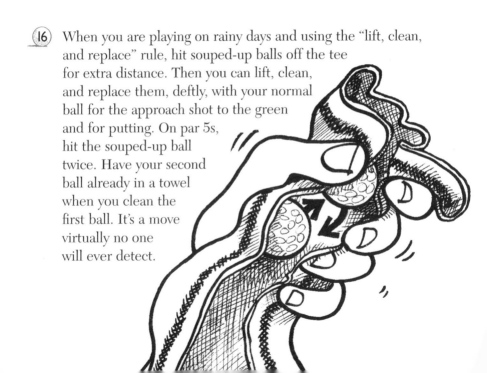

(17) When your opponent is putting first and your ball is on the same line, he may ask you to move your spot either left or right so that the coin does not interfere with the roll of his ball. This is done by aligning the original spot with some background feature such as a tree trunk, and moving the coin from the toe of the putter back to the heel. You can get your ball significantly closer to the hole by aligning the spot forward of its original position, and then meticulously aligning with yet another forward marker as you ostensibly align it with the original marker. Because people are always concentrating so deeply on their own putts, no one is ever going to notice, as long as you don't move a three-foot putt two feet.

(18) Know the rules of golf and always use them to your advantage. If your opponent is about to commit a breach of the rules, don't tell him until he's done it. Then, in a hesitant and humble voice, tell him that he's broken a rule. Say that you think he should know about this for the future. Say that he should carry a rule book in his bag. Make all the right ethical and moral statements before saying, "By the way, that's an automatic two-stroke penalty, so you have lost the hole."

(19) Always have a regular caddie, and always tip him well. It will keep him on your side all of the time. And maybe he'll carry a spare ball in a pocket with a hole just big enough to squeeze it through. This comes in handy when looking for a ball that is in the thick of the woods. What a welcome relief it is to hear your caddie say: "Boss, you were playing a Maxfli 3, right? Here it is." Naturally your lie will be obstacle-free and clean as a whistle. Caddies can also jiggle coins, cough, and wear reflective watches, taking the onus off you.

(20) Call your opponent at five o'clock in the morning to remind him of the game you have at noon. It will be difficult for him to get back to sleep. If he asks you why you're calling at that hour, say you forgot what time zone he was in. Hopefully he'll be too dazed to realize that he's right next door. This is a ploy to be used by sound sleepers only.

Well-Known Bettors

Titanic Thompson

While golf gambling has existed since the first shepherds tried to roll stones into holes 500 years ago, it was Titanic Thompson who brought this art form to life in the 1920s and 1930s. Alvin C. "Titanic" Thompson was a professional golfer, but he was much more of a professional gambler. He bet on golf, cards, ponies—anything for the action. He'd even bet hotel clerks that he could throw his key into the key box behind the desk in order to get a free room.

Once while playing a money match (the only type he ever played), he bet a competitor that a dog in a backyard that adjoined the course would bark before anyone in their group hit their next shot. The catch? Keen-sighted Thompson had just observed a rabbit about to cross the dog's line of vision. Another time he won $12,000 in a match in Galveston by linking together fifty side bets. Above all, Thompson was the epitome of the gambler: He showed no mercy to anyone.

Sam Snead

Slammin' Sam Snead is one of the game's immortals, having won everything there was to win in golf except the U.S. Open. But Snead was also known as one of golf's preeminent gamblers. His games at the Meadow Brook Club on Long Island were for nothing less than $3,000, a rather healthy sum in the 1930s. Snead was of the era when professionals not only gambled their own money, but were the objects of wagering themselves.

In the late '30s, Snead once played an arranged match against the pro at the Havana, Cuba, Country Club with at least $100,000 in wagers on the line. Snead won the 36-hole match and got out of Cuba in a hurry, afraid the dictator Batista's men, who had money on his opponent, would be chasing him down. As Snead once said, "I tried to quit gambling once, but it was about as much use as kicking a hog barefoot."

Lee Trevino

Three decades ago, a hustling driving range pro from Texas popped up on the PGA Tour and never went away. Before he got on tour, virtually the only money that Lee Trevino ever made was by gambling. He's the author of the immortal quote, "Gambling is when you're playing for $5 and you've got $2 in your pocket." Trevino won a lot of those $5 bets, including matches against suckers who didn't know about his proficiency with a Dr Pepper bottle.

He would agree to tee off with the Dr Pepper bottle, hitting "fungo style," and the naive or the just plain stupid would jump at the bet. The thing was, he had practiced using that bottle thousands of times and had his swing with it grooved as if it were today's Big Bertha.

Al Besselink

Known as "Bessie," Al Besselink would spend upward of $100,000 a year traveling the PGA Tour back in the 1950s, when he never made more than $20,000 in purse money. Bessie lived large because he bet large, and when he played in Las Vegas, it was as close to heaven as he could get.

After a third-place finish in the Masters tournament in 1953, he got an invitation to play in the original Tournament of Champions in Las Vegas. The deal included a free suite, free caddie, all expenses, and $1,000 to boot. He started to bet the bookies that he would win, at odds of 30 to 1 and more. He led the first round, the second round, and the third round. Before he teed off on Sunday, panicky bookies had already settled bets with him to the tune of $50,000. He went on to win the tournament and its first prize of $10,000. Not just a money grubber, he donated half the winner's check to the Walter Winchell–Damon Runyon Cancer Fund in the name of Babe Zaharias.

Bobby Riggs

Most people know Bobby Riggs as a tennis player, and a pretty good one in his prime. His most defining moment in tennis came when he challenged Billy Jean King to a match, which was played at the Astrodome in Houston. He lost.

But he won big on the golf course almost all his life. At his home club on Long Island, he pulled off his biggest betting coup of all time. Riggs was a master at "talking bets up," that is, getting someone to play for more than they originally agreed to by cajoling them into various side bets as the round progressed. If his pigeon wasn't playing well he might softly suggest, "Maybe if you had a little more money riding you would concentrate better." On this particular day, in a match that started out with a loss potential of maybe $500, Riggs got to the ego of his pigeon so deeply that the pigeon eventually lost his house and his business to Riggs in that one afternoon.

Lanny Wadkins

For years Lanny Wadkins was known as the PGA Tour's "leading money winner on Tuesday." That's because Tuesday is usually when the pros play their serious practice rounds before a tournament. Wadkins would rather have not practiced at all than played without some kind of bet at stake.

He played most regularly with Arnold Palmer, Ray Floyd, and Lee Trevino—all top names that loved the action as much as he did. With $100 Nassaus going against everybody, and presses and some side bets as well, Wadkins often enjoyed a $1,000 practice day—sometimes double that amount.

Wadkins was always known as one of the game's most aggressive players. He had little tolerance for the patience game that is modern professional golf. He would fire at every pin rather than play conservatively, a trait he simply carried over from his Tuesday competitions.

The Betting
Games

The Game: The Nassau Bet

This is the most common four-ball bet extant. Begun at the Nassau Country Club on Long Island around the turn of the century, the Nassau bet is usually a match play of teams of two vying for the three betting points—winning the front nine, the back nine, and the overall eighteen. Handicaps can be used, with one team giving the other the fewest strokes possible. It's usually $5 per man, meaning that if you win all three bets, each player on the winning team gets $15. Additionally, more money is on the line if a trailing team decides to press. Often pressing, closing out the first bet and creating a double-down bet on the remaining holes, is automatic when a team falls two down on the front nine or back nine. A press can be made for the front nine or the entire eighteen. If the team falls a further two holes down, it can also add a second press. Appoint the neatest person in the group to keep score. While the bet is most often equal on each betting point, you will find players who play "four ways" or even "six ways." Four ways is automatically doubling the bet on the back nine. Six ways is doubling the back nine and tripling the match bet.

The Edge

Because this game is played with handicaps, arrange to have the best high handicapper you can find as your partner. A player who has, say, a 14 handicap achieved by making eight pars and several double and triple bogeys would make an excellent partner because he is capable of shooting many more pars (which will net birdies with the handicap) than his handicap would indicate. And since it's match play, the total score doesn't matter, anyway.

The Game: Bingo, Bango, Bongo

No, this is not the latest dance craze. It's a fairly common game that puts value on the long game, the short game, and putting. Three points are possible on each hole: The first point goes to the player hitting the green in the fewest number of strokes; the second goes to the player closest to the pin after everyone is on the green; the third goes to the person with the lowest total score on the hole. Handicaps can be used, but they only apply to the last point. On par-3 holes, you can award two points for closest to the pin and one point for fewest strokes. Add up the points at the end of the round. The player who has the most collects the difference between his total and each of the other players at the agreed-upon per-point price.

The Edge

If you're a good chipper and putter, this is a good game to play against players who are slightly better from tee to green than you are. They may win the first point more often, but the odds will be in your favor for the second and third points. A sneaky way to increase your odds is by getting the other players to agree that the third point goes to the player who gets it in the hole first, regardless of the number of strokes it takes. This way, even if your score would put you out of play for the final point, you can try to maneuver the ball on the green so that you set yourself up to putt first, but from a makable distance.

The Game: Backgammon

Backgammon can be played one-on-one or pair-on-pair. It's loosely based on the casino game and doubling up the bets at any time is the object here. You may play for $1, $2, or $5 a hole, but before a hole is completed, a player or team may double the bet if they think they have an advantage—or want to test the choke quotient of their opponents. When one team calls double, the other team may double back. The other team may also decline the double, but in doing so automatically owes the doubling team half the original bet and may not itself double at any later point in the hole.

The Edge

Normally, a double has to be called before the play has been made. A sneaky way to get around this is to double while your opponent's ball is in the air and headed out of bounds. This aspect of the game might not be discussed at the first tee, and don't bring it up yourself. Just wait for the time that such a wayward shot might maximize a bet, such as when a team has doubled back and the stakes are four times the original. This tactic is to be used sparingly and wisely, and be prepared for an argument. Just say, "Since we didn't prohibit it to begin with, then it's got to be a legal double."

The Game: Worse Ball

This is a great game to play against a good player, if he's stupid enough to take you up on it. The good player has to hit two balls from every position, starting at the tee, and play the worse one until he finally holes out. That means if he hits a dynamite shot, he'll have to discard it and try to hit another one, which can feed his frustration in a hurry. Begin by deciding if there are any strokes involved. If the good player is smart, he'll ask that your handicap allotment be cut in half, at least. Hold out for as many strokes as you can get.

The Edge

You have to find someone with a big ego and a small brain to play this game, because it's almost a lock. This is especially true if you manage to convince the sucker to play eighteen holes. In reality, he will be playing thirty-six holes, since he must hit every shot twice until he gets it on the green, and he's likely to run out of energy and patience after the first nine holes. While putting is often left out of the equation, don't be afraid to ask that he take two putts on every green. That means if he holes out the first one, it doesn't count and he must hole out the second one to achieve the same score.

Unfortunately, this is a game you can play only once against someone, unless you have looked at a CAT scan of his head and see nothing whatsoever.

The Game: Criers and Whiners

A.K.A. "No Alibis and Replay," this is another good game for milking your more talented opponent's ego. It requires the better player to replay shots on demand, with the number of replays determined by the difference in handicap strokes between the bettors. If your handicap is 16 and his is 8, then you would negotiate for eight replays. If you've got a player that is always crying and whining about the fact that he would hit a better shot if he had a second chance, this is a great game. You can play this bet hole-by-hole or in the Nassau bet form.

The Edge

When calling replays, look to call back good drives on the tough driving holes and great approach shots on the toughest of the greens. It's a good idea, at the start, not to begin using your replay strokes if you don't absolutely have to. If you are down by two holes after six, then start using them, but hold off as long as possible. The longer you can hold off, the more pressure you are putting on your opponent, who will be wracked with the conflicting emotions of comfort that he's not losing and dread that he will start having to replay a bunch of shots soon. If there is a large difference between handicaps, say a 20 up against a 2,

2.

then ask not only for eighteen replays of his shots, but an additional amount of replays of your own bad shots. You'll get a big argument, but hey, don't we love this kind of thing?

The Game: Vegas

Gawd, you gotta love this game, which goes right back to the *Caddyshack* days. If you feel faint over a $1 bet at a roulette table, don't play this game. In fact, don't gamble at all because you'll just lose friends and make enemies faster than if you took a job with the IRS.

While there are many variations of this game, the basics are that you play two against two with each pair's score bundled. The difference between the bundled scores is the money won or lost. Bundling means that if you and your partner have a four and five on a hole, your score is forty-five. If your opponents' have a five and six, they have a fifty-six. That's an eleven-point difference and is multiplied by the unit value of the points, be they $1 or $10. All sorts of doubling and tripling and quadrupling can take place in advance, like doubling when a player makes a birdie, or tripling on an eagle, or quadrupling when both teammates make birdie.

The Edge

As always, you want to pick your partner wisely, since it's the single best tactic to winning any game. In this game, a steady, unspectacular player who makes par and seldom worse than bogey can team up with an erratic player who nonetheless is capable of some spectacular play. His upside—the fact that he can make a couple of birdies and some pars—has far more impact than his downside—where he makes a double or triple bogey—since those numbers will generally be the second ones in the score bundle. However, if you are playing reversals, whereby your opponents birdie a hole, double the bet, and require that your highest score be put first, then the erratic player can be a liability.

The Game: Scotch (Alternate Shot)

In a foursome, it's one twosome against the other. And in a threesome, it's a twosome against a single, switching pairs every six holes. Each player in a twosome takes turns hitting shots. One player drives, the other hits the approach; the first one putts, the second putts; and so on. When the pair's last putt is holed, the other player is the one who tees off on the next hole. There is no designated driver, or alternating order of who hits tee shots. It's the player who didn't make the last putt. In the threesome version, you add up holes won as a single and those won with a partner. Whoever has the highest total is the overall winner, getting the unit difference between his total and each of his partners.

The Edge

In the foursome, it's important to figure out which player in your pairing is the better putter, because those are the players that usually determine the outcome. You want that player taking as many first putts as possible. The good putting partner should be driving on par-4 holes, hitting second shots on par 5s, and making the first putts on par 3s. This takes some scorecard analyzing to determine which holes are which, so stall for time before teeing off in order to make your best possible guess. Call the Psychic Friends Network if you have to.

Pay attention to this: There may be situations in which the good putter is faced with hitting a very troublesome shot to the green. Rather than risking that shot, which may leave you either with a horribly long putt or some sort of dreaded recovery shot, the good putter should consider laying up. This will allow his partner the easiest possible approach shot and give him the best chance to make the putt.

The Game: Arnies and Jacks

This can be a game unto itself or a side bet to any number of other games, played one-on-one or pair-against-pair. It's based on Arnold Palmer and Jack Nicklaus when they were in the prime of their careers. "Arnies" are pars made without a ball ever touching the fairway, double units for birdies. "Jacks" are pars made with the longest drive, double units for birdies. Both sides can be eligible for both bets on the same holes. Usually, par 3s aren't counted in any way, except perhaps for Arnies after missing the green.

The Edge

If you are a big, strong player, this is the game for you. If you hit long, you have a leg up on the Jacks. And if you're long, you're obviously strong, which helps tremendously on the Arnies side of the bet. In fact, if you are long and strong and have a reasonable touch with the putter, don't even try to hit the fairway. You'll be in line to clean up on both bets. If you happen to hit the fairway, it's just a tough break.

Play this game alongside a Vegas. The combinations—and the gut checks—will be endless. Besides, if you're sneaky enough or have a caddie personally beholden to you, you can always "find" your ball in the rough well ahead of your opponent.

The Game: Cross Country

This is a six-o'clock-at-night game for at least four players who have had at least two beers each, because that's what makes it fun. The object is to play from the tee of one hole to the green of another, ideally the longest stretch across the entire golf course. It might be a mile from the third tee to the fifteenth green, and whoever gets there by whatever route in the fewest number of strokes wins. The player with the least number of strokes either collects money from a set pot of, say, $10 per man, or a set value per unit of strokes between himself and each of the other players. The first wagering method is far easier and presents fewer temptations to cheat. If you really want to make this interesting, play from one golf course to another.

The Edge

This can go to the player who knows in advance certain advantageous routes, particularly if you declare that no out-of-bounds rules apply. Then you might be able to cut across the yard of someone dumb enough to own a home on a golf course in a tract separating two holes.

Or you could flag down a course worker out cleaning up and ask if you might pitch your ball into the back of his utility cart…which he then drives to the target green. The worker can attest that you played only one shot into the cart, and since it isn't your equipment, you don't get penalized. That might be a little much for your opponents to take, but this is a game of creativity as well as skill. If playing from course to course, try pitching one onto a public bus and riding the ball to the next course.

The Game: Snake

This is one simple game that is usually played on the side with other games. The object here is not to three-putt. If you do, you take possession of "the snake" and you don't lose it until someone else three-putts. For each hole that you possess the snake, you pay each of your partners a set amount, such as $1 apiece. If you are in possession of the snake and hole a chip shot, bunker shot, pitch shot, or any kind of fluky shot from off the green, you can either declare your bets canceled, or get three bucks apiece from each player, whichever is most beneficial for you. From the start of the round, carry over the snake-bet money from hole to hole and watch the first person to three-putt get snakebit.

The Edge

Players who are good chippers, pitchers, and sand players love this game, because they seldom three-putt. In fact, there may be certain situations toward the end of a round where you might miss the green intentionally, putting yourself in position for an easy up-and-down and eliminating the possibility of a three-putt. This could be true early on, as well, when a lot of carryovers are at stake.

The Game: Captain and Crew

Best played by a foursome or more, this is a game of ruthless business opportunity. At the first tee, the players determine what rotation they will each go in as Captain. You can play "rock, paper, scissors," tic-tac-toe, or use any other silly method to determine the order. If you have to, go from highest handicap to lowest.

The Captain is the first player to tee off on a hole, and gets to choose a crew member/partner based on the drives of the other players. That choice can be made either when all the shots are hit, or the Captain can make a choice either to accept or reject a crew member after each tee shot—a testy alternative. Best ball of the group wins the hole. As Captain, you can win outright or you can win if your crew member wins the hole. If a single player wins a hole, his bet can be doubled. A Captain can also choose to play alone, with the bets doubled. After sixteen holes, the rotation runs out, and the player who is trailing in the betting gets to be the Captain on seventeen and eighteen.

The Edge

Do not let friendship or compassion enter into your thinking about this game. Take the best shot, take the best player, or don't take anyone, all based on what you think is best for you. This is true in all golf gambling; it's just doubled up, so to speak, for this game. All things being equal, and especially on par 3s, pick the best putter. If the best putter is marginally behind the player with the best drive, stick with the best putter. This is also a good game for conniving with another player, who plays his worst when selected by the two other players, and plays his best with you, and vice versa. A good game for dirty rotten scoundrels.

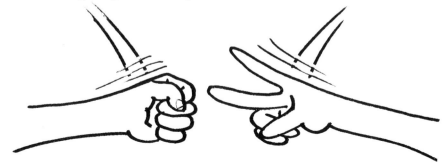

The Game: Yardages

This is a very simple game that can become very expensive. Played between singles or pairs, winners get a unit per yard for each hole they win. If you are playing $1 units, and you win a 560-yard par 5, you win $1 per yard, or $560. Did you just get a little wobbly, like you were looking down at the street from the top of the World Trade Center? Of course, you could play for a penny or a nickel or a dime a yard, but that's for the meek and the miserable.

Add some interest by allowing a trailing team to start doubling the stakes on any hole on the back nine. Trailers are allowed to double the stakes on any par 3. Halved holes are carried over, so that if three straight par 4s are halved, you're talking serious throw-up money on the subsequent hole.

A particularly humiliating way to make up for lost money is asking to play from the ladies' tee. If you win, you win the yardage units from that tee. If you lose, you lose the yardage units from back on the men's tee, plus the difference between the men's and ladies' tees. If you halve the hole, you still owe your opponent the yardage between the tees. A leading opponent can require you to play from the ladies' tee, in a blatant attempt at humiliation, but if he halves the hole, you win double the yardage difference. If he loses, you win the yardage from the back tee, plus double the yardage between tees.

The Edge

There isn't one, unless you are a much bigger hitter, which gives you the edge on long par-3 and par-4 holes. If you are feeling good about your game and are up on your opponents early, send them to the ladies' tee. This is especially effective for par-3 and par-5 holes where the yardage difference isn't that significant to a bigger hitter. You want the humiliation factor to set in early. And if you should win the hole with your opponents playing the ladies' markers, send them right back up there again. Humiliation, more than the money, might be the biggest pressure factor going.

The Game: Chugging, or Down the Hatch

First, do not play this game while using golf carts. Second, do not play this game and then drive home. If you do not have a designated driver, an angry spouse to pick you up, or a local cabby used to your slurred phone calls, then simply do not play this game ever, ever, ever. Now then, chugging tests your equilibrium, your bladder, and the size of your hollow leg. Simply put, if you win a hole, you must chug down a small beer before play on the next hole is completed. If you don't finish your beer before the next hole is played, you lose that hole automatically. This is a wonderful game for those who can drink beer all day. It's really an overlay, an added dimension to any other game you wish to play. And you win an extra unit or two if you go eighteen holes without going to the bathroom.

The Edge

Unless your opponent is actually clever enough to require you to pop a can in front of him, pour out the good beer in your cans (save it in the fridge for poker games) and fill up your beer cans with non-alcoholic brews. This requires some deftness on your part. To make this one work, you'll have to hit a poor shot now and then, stumble walking down the fairway occasionally, and maybe give up the bonus units for not relieving yourself.

The Game: Piggy Bank

Here you play for points on the holes, usually setting a low value for each of the first six holes, a higher value for the next six, and the highest value for the final six holes. For every par, you earn the determined point value. A birdie doubles the number of points. A bogey is nothing, but a double bogey eliminates all points you've accumulated unless you've put them in the bank. For example, after winning 100 points, you may decide to put them in the bank before you play a particularly difficult hole. If you make double bogey, those points can't be lost, but you don't start earning any points again until the hole after the hole on which you make your next par. You can also decide on the first tee whether a triple bogey causes you to lose half the points in the bank, and a quadruple bogey causes you to lose them all. The player with the most points after eighteen holes wins all the money in the kitty, or the difference in units between his score and each of the other players'.

The Edge

The game is one where better players can have a distinct advantage. Here, you can play your own game, rather than react to the other players, and par is an extremely good score. You don't have to try to do anything spectacular. And if you are confident in your game, you don't have to bank any of the points, leaving them out there to accumulate freely without giving up the opportunity to win points on a hole because you're waiting for your next par. The good player should try to overlay this game on top of a basic Nassau. The more games a good player has going, the better off he will be.

The Game: Bridge

Okay, so this is a pretty lame name for a game. But it has to do with bidding on holes, pair against pair. The pair winning the coin flip for honors on the first tee is the first pair to bid on a hole. The bid is based on the total score of both players, but it cannot exceed one over par for players with combined handicaps of 19 or less, two over for players with combined handicaps of between 20 and 29 strokes, or three over for combined handicaps that are 30 and above. Let's say the first hole is a par 4 and a team of good players bids eight, which means that a combined score of eight or less wins the bet regardless of how the other team plays. The opponents can accept the bid, make an even lower bid, and can even double the bet itself if they think there is a good chance the first pair won't make it. If a team comes in under its bid—let's say makes a seven after bidding eight—it wins double the bet. If it comes in two under the bid, it wins quadruple.

The Edge

Always go for a low bid, because you want to control your own destiny as much as possible. Also, since handicap strokes are figured into the bidding, take these into consideration on any given hole when making a bid. Even though the more difficult the hole, the more strokes, it makes it easier to set a realistic bid. The pair with more strokes can almost always make their bids or force a team with fewer strokes to make a foolish play for a lower bid. This game may sound dull, but it can be extremely interesting, especially when two players are arguing over a bid. If the argument results in a lower bid, double it, because the consequences of the argument almost always carry over into the way a person plays.

The Game: Par 3 Madness

A special game for a special hole in special circumstances. The object of this game is simple: getting the ball onto the green. Select the toughest par 3 you can find, and get a group of at least eight players together. A hole longer than 200 yards, across water with wind blowing around 60 m.p.h., is perfect. Get everybody out to the hole in golf carts, bringing along extra beer. For each game of Madness, you ante up a set amount—maybe $5 per player—and put it in the kitty. Each player gets one swing and one chance to put a ball on the green. If only one player hits the green, he wins. If two or more players hit the green, the winner is the one closest to the hole. Then you start over again and keep going until night falls or the club pro comes out and chases you away with the shotgun he usually fires at the start of tournaments.

The Edge

If you can get away with it, drop one of your balls in the hole well in advance of playing this game. Then, as night falls and vision becomes impaired by lack of light and no lack of lite beer, tee a ball up and whack it with at least three extra clubs, making sure that the backdrop to the green isn't a stand of trees where the sound of the ball driving through the leaves and the limbs will be a dead giveaway. "Man, that was the best swing I've made this year," you declare. "It was right on the stick." You say this, of course, after your first ball is out of sight and out of mind. Then you state that you think you made it. And, lo and behold, there it is. Try to get everyone to agree in advance that they owe you 10 times the bet if there is a hole-in-one.

If you actually win this bet, get out of town fast. First, because somebody's probably hunting you down; second, because if no one is hunting you down, these people must be so dumb as to be contagious.

The Game: Skins

This has become the most famous of all betting games because of the long-running Skins Game, a perennial television favorite on Thanksgiving weekend, in which top pros go at each other without risking a cent of their own money. It should be played as a foursome, each player against everybody else, with the object to win a hole outright. That's known as a "skin." Each player contributes a unit value for each of eighteen holes. At a dollar a player per hole, there's a total of $72. A skin is therefore equal to $4 a hole. If two or more players tie on a hole,

then that skin carries over to the next one, and the skins continue to carry over until someone finally wins a hole outright.

The Edge

It goes to the player with a high handicap, since he can win a disproportionate amount of money on one hole when there has been a significant buildup of carryovers. But, of course, you should never volunteer this information. It is especially good to keep your mouth shut around neophyte gamblers who bring passion to the betting game but no brains. They might foolishly allow you to use your full handicap rather than talking you down to a half, which is customary.

The Game: Pick Up Sticks

You should really like this game because it allows you to disenfranchise players from their favorite clubs. To be good at the game not only requires the skill to win more holes than your opponent, but knowledge of the requirements of the course and your opponent's best club or group of clubs.

Here's how it works: The basic betting game is hole-by-hole with a unit value per hole. If you lose a hole, you get to take a club out of your opponent's bag. You can also take a club out of the opponent's bag by winning a hole with a birdie. The putter is sometimes considered immune, but that's wimping out—don't protect any clubs. Also, while a variation of the game allows a player to win his clubs back, don't play that way, either. That's a double wimp-out.

The Edge

Take the putter first, followed by the pitching wedge and the short irons. Don't take the longer clubs, like the driver or the 2-iron, because those don't tend to be the average player's best clubs, anyhow. Though if you know that a player can't play a lick without his driver, you might go for that first, followed by the putter. A great variation: Instead of removing a specific club, require your opponent to play with the comparable club in your bag. There's nothing better to screw up somebody's swing than to give him a different club in the middle of a round. Chances are he might not be able to make a confident swing the rest of the day after getting diseased by your club.

The Game: Master of Disaster

The object of this game is to collect the fewest number of points in a round, but not necessarily shoot the lowest score, though Master of Disaster can be overlaid onto other games. Basically, points are given for players who lose balls, hit them out of bounds, or end up in fairway bunkers, green side bunkers, or water hazards. Points are also given for three-putt greens and for whiffing a ball, or for topping a teed-up ball. You might want to double up some forms of trouble points, like leaving a shot in a bunker or hitting the next shot into another form of trouble. You might want to reduce points for saving par out of a bunker, or saving double points by making birdie. The player with the fewest points wins a set amount of units for each point of difference between himself and his opponent or opponents.

The Edge

If you are playing against one player, try to set up the game on a course that plays to his weaknesses, your strengths, or both, if possible. For instance, if there tends to be a lot of trouble to the right side of the majority of holes on one course, and your opponent is a slicer, then try to have more points awarded for the hazards that are on that side of the course. Make up a list in advance, and hand it to your opponent, asking if everything is okay by him. Chances are he'll be so impressed that he will neglect to see that the points are set up against his specific game. If he's a bad putter, quadruple the three-putt points against all others—assuming you don't three-putt very often.

The Game: String

This is one of the most interesting, if little played, gambling gimmicks there is. You can choose to play any sort of game you like, because string is a rescue technique and not an actual bet. Nonetheless, creative use of the string can help you win matches. You need matching lengths of string and a pair of scissors per player to use this gimmick. Everybody starts out with a set length of string, let's say fifteen feet. Players may use any length of string, up to the maximum, to move the ball in any direction, including forward. You may use it to move yourself out of a sandtrap and onto a green, or out of a water hazard to where you can clearly identify your ball on dry land. The catch is you must cut off and discard the length of string used, leaving you with less and less each time.

The Edge

Try to save as much string as possible until the final holes where there may be a lot of money on the line. Do this when you are playing skins. Also consider small moves early in the round, such as when you might be able to dramatically improve your lie in the fairway after it has come to rest in an old divot. By using two inches of string, you might improve your chances for a good shot by 50 percent. For the unscrupulous, carry a five-foot length of string in your other back pocket and whip it out when you get below that length with your original string. Also, never play this game against magicians, who, with slight of hand, can double up the string while appearing to cut it.

The Game: Bogey

This is a game for good players, which leaves 99 percent of us out. Pros like Lee Trevino like this game, since it puts a lot of pressure on a player right from the start. Basically, the first player to bogey a hole carries the bogeyman label until another player makes bogey. If two players bogey the same hole, there is no blood. A player owes the other players a unit a hole, starting on the hole he bogeyed, until another player makes bogey to become the new bogeyman. If in doubt, it's the bogeyman who gets the short end of the stick: If the bogeyman and another player bogey the same hole, the label doesn't transfer. Ditto if two opponents bogey the same hole—the bogeyman's still the bogeyman.

In a variation, the bogeyman can lose the label by making a birdie. The bogeyman can also owe double units to an opponent player who makes a birdie. For added pressure, double the bets on the second hole that the bogeyman carries the label, triple them on the third hole, and so forth.

Not-so-good players can play Double Bogey, though that just sounds a bit too amateurish.

The Edge

Any good player wants this kind of a bet. He can play conservatively and still win. It's kind of like the U.S. Open in that it rewards patience much more so than risk. If you are the one suggesting the game, be sure to assess the bogey status of the holes early in the round. If there is a hole on the course you're playing that gives you trouble, then maybe you want to pass on the game since you might be carrying the bogeyman label early. Then again, if you think your opponents will be picking up early bogeys based on how they play certain holes, go for it. The first player to make bogey carries the most pressure.

The Game: Bobby Jones

This presents a real challenge to the good player, and a really good chance for some extra cash for the high handicapper. In this game, the better player has to play his second shot from where his opponent's tee shot came to rest, and vice versa. The game requires a certain amount of trust, or a certain amount of skulduggery. In other words, both players are trusting that the other player is trying to hit his best possible tee shot. That might be too much to ask anyone familiar with all the scamming going on in golf, but let's assume that occasionally there really is honor among thieves. And if you lack that honor in too obvious a manner, you'll probably get called for tanking anyway, which means your opponent will receive a two-club-length relief from where your shot ends up.

The high handicapper will still get some handicap strokes, though he will have to work hard to get them. Play any sort of game you want with this sort of gimmick. Shots into hazards or that incur penalty strokes do not count and must be played again.

The Edge

For the better player, try to subtly hit shots that place the higher handicapper in more jeopardy than he might initially realize. For instance, if there is a fairway bunker complex out there on a par 5 or long par 4, try to curve a ball into it, since high handicappers have much more difficulty with sand than the better players. You have to do this cautiously since the high handicapper, sensing you are tanking, can call it on any tee shot. For the higher handicapper, it's clear that tee shots behind trees or into deep rough are the best, but the better player can also declare tanking, so you must do this wisely.

The Game: Monopoly

If you are a member of a private club, or a public course player who plays the same course most of the time, this is the game for you. Monopoly, just like the original board game, is best played long-term—over the length of the entire season, or at least ten rounds. Never heard of it? That's because it's being introduced here as a bonus for the truly ill players. These are players who are one step removed from Gamblers Anonymous or who perhaps are even card-carrying members.

Starting with the first round of the year, each hole is a property. The object is to win holes, which you own until your opponents wrest them away from you. When you own a hole, you charge rent on it each time your opponent lands on it without winning it himself. Rents are predetermined and range from the highest at the number 1 and 2 handicap holes (Park Place and Broadway), to the lowest at the number 17 and 18 handicap holes (Mediterranean and Baltic). You may build a house on an owned hole each subsequent time you win the hole, and charge double the rent for each house up to a total of four houses. When your opponent wins the hole back, all the houses are wiped out. This takes a lot of bookkeeping, but since you are miserably obsessed with golf to begin with, what's a little more time invested in keeping score? This is a major overlay game.

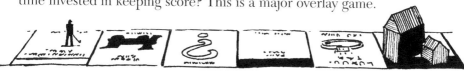

The Edge

Put all your resources into winning the more difficult holes, since they are the big-time payoffs. This must really be played even up, since allotting handicap strokes gives the weaker player the better part of the deal when it comes to the more difficult, high-rent holes. Of course, if your opponent doesn't say anything about it, don't bring it up if you are getting strokes from him. Take the strokes on the tough holes and laugh all the way to the bank.

The Game: Ringer

This is another game to be played over more than one round and overlaid on other games. In Ringer, you play a set number of rounds, then take your best score on each hole and add up the total. Whoever has the low—or ringer—score wins. You may also add a match play function to this, comparing individual holes and who the winner is of each. The final ringer scorecard can be used to play any number of games you didn't realize you were playing in the first place.

The Edge

While this is a game that really should be played by golfers of similar handicaps, again don't hesitate to take strokes if a much better player doesn't say anything about cutting those strokes down by a half or three quarters. This can be customary in this game since you have several shots at achieving a good score on a hole before the handicaps are ever figured in. The less proficient player has a decided advantage here if the better player doesn't cut his handicap strokes.

The Game: War

Here you get to ignore the rules of golf completely insofar as they apply to gentlemanly conduct. You see, in War you may do anything to an opponent's ball. Try it this way: If you have a handicap that's two shots higher than your opponents, instead of taking them as strokes, you employ them as acts of war. You may kick a ball into a bunker or hazard, run it down with your golf cart, or merely step on it. You may throw it as far as you like in any direction, including into ponds and backyards that are out of bounds. This is really rotten business, this one. You can use these acts of war on any given hole, or only at the hole in which you would normally receive the handicap shot. This must be decided before the start of the round. Play any game you like with this gimmick.

The Edge

If you are getting strokes, try to use them on any given hole rather than on the holes where the handicap would normally apply. This way you can save them for when you really need them. A really good technique to use late in a round is to step on a ball in a bunker. This turns what might be an easy shot for the better player into a crapshoot.

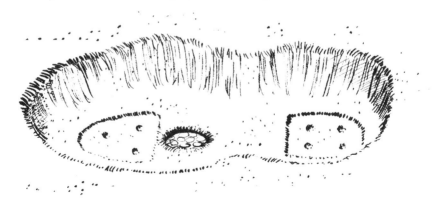

ABOUT THE AUTHOR

Jay Willi (Jeff Williams) turned eligible for the Senior Tour in 1997, becoming 50 on April 15, tax day. Since the age of 13, he has sought the elusive golf swing with virtually no success. He realized early on that he would earn far more money writing about golf than playing it.

He has won awards for golf writing, tennis writing, and hockey writing as a senior writer for *Newsday,* the nation's sixth largest newspaper. He is also a widely circulated magazine writer, appearing regularly in *Cigar Aficionado, Senior Golfer, Golf Magazine, Tour Magazine, The Major Series*, and several other publications.

Williams lives with his wife Randal and three children, Cameron, Caitlin, and Samantha, in Huntington, New York.

This is his first book.